Kids are Dicks. Part 1

A gonzo parenting book

By Paul E Di Cintio

This is a work of humour and fiction. Names, characters, places, and incidents either are the product of the author's imagination or are used fictitiously. Any resemblance to actual persons, apart from Jason, living or dead, events or locales is entirely coincidental.

For more information, address: hello@kidsaredicks.net

First paperback edition September 2024.

Book design by Paul E Di Cintio
Illustrations by Spartac Cebanu

ISBN 978-0-646-89338-9 (paperback)
Also available in ebook

www.kidsaredicks.net
Instagram @kids_are_dicks
X/Twitter @kids_r_dicks

Dedication

To my parents Enzo and Maria who taught me to parent, and to my wonderful son Raphael Lupe 'Super Loops' 'Fruity Loops' 'Loops' 'Wayan' 'Handsome' Di Cintio who is the best companion anyone could ask for. You fill my life with joy.

Preface

PLEASE READ THIS! I really need you to read this, because this is the part where I make excuses for all the advice I'm about to give – and explain why you should ignore that advice. It's probably best to return the book before you dog-ear the pages and can't get your money back.

Let me begin with this: I have absolutely no qualifications in child development or child psychology. I did work at after-school care in my teens, I did my share of babysitting and I do have an odd connection with kids. Kids just like me – perhaps because I have fun with them, treat them as equals, still love to play and am not afraid to be a fool.

Most of the advice I'm going to impart is based on being a parent, Montessori teachings, the best parental book I ever read called The Discipline Book by William and Martha Sears, Instagram and TikTok, so proceed with caution. Fortunately, less wisdom has been derived from Instagram and TikTok, but I must admit I get a few pearls from those formats, too.

I just love being a parent. I thought even prior to becoming a parent that I was born to be a parent. It's just a very easy thing for me. I hope that what lies ahead will help you, and make it easy, too.

I co-parent but have always been a single parent of the most wonderful boy, who at the time of writing this is fifteen years old. He suggested to me that I should write a parenting book, and if that's not the most wonderful thing to hear from a child, then I don't know what is. My son even came up with the title as I have been known to say it a lot over the years.

I wanted to preface this book by letting you know my situation and that my advice stems from my position, and I think that some, all, or everything of what I lay before you may not be applicable to everyone. My advice does come from the position of someone who is privileged. I'm not talking Beverly hills – I mean I live in an apartment in a nice, leafy, safe, inner-city suburb. I can't afford to own a small house in the area. I do not own a holiday house. I am a medium-income earner with a fun job, living in one of the best and safest cities in the world: Melbourne, Australia. I must acknowledge the wonderful job my loving parents did along with my caring brothers and extended family, who together have given me a stable base to grow and learn from. It's been a secure and enriching life with so many opportunities presented to me. My position enables me to travel, experience culture, have time off, visit galleries and afford cultural activities. I'm not trying to boast – just to say that I am grateful for these opportunities, knowing that they are not the same for all.

I am also the parent of a regular kid and appreciate that children are all different and that your situation will not be the same as mine, so please take that into account. I do believe children are born with unique traits, and there isn't a 'one size fits all' solution. Parents face their own unique challenges. I tip my hat to you all.

I also want to acknowledge that some of my advice can be contradictory and sometimes controversial, so you feel free to take what you want. Feedback and discussion are welcomed, and I won't be surprised if this is picked apart and thrown back at me; but hey, writing a book is being vulnerable, especially on a topic which is so personal.

I am not a serious person, and although I'm pushing 50 years of age, I have not lost the inner child. I have never written a book, and I'm Australian, so I tend to write loosely, use inappropriate words and can be blunt – so there.

I do hope you enjoy it. I did write it to share my ideas and amuse, but mainly for my son. The manner in which I write is not too dissimilar to the way I communicate with my son. I hope that this book may help you be a better parent in some way, and hopefully fewer kids will be dicks.

Oh, oh, oh – 'dicks', is short for 'dickheads', which we use in Australia as a gender-neutral description for someone who is annoying. Don't have annoying children, 'cause those children are annoying.

Mission statement

I am pretty sure I came up with it myself, having a mission statement for parenting. I was educated in business studies at university, where it's typical for a corporation to have a mission statement: a guiding aim for the company. I'm not sure why this is not adopted by parents across the world. Isn't it a great idea to have a goal in mind when raising a child? My mission statement is: 'To rear an independent, empathetic child who loves learning.' I know it's super simple – not many words – yet it has guided my parenting so much over the years.

It reminds me that even when it takes him a long time to get dressed in the morning, I just have to deal with it, because it's fostering independence. Do I make his bed for him? No, because that breeds co-dependency. Do I buy him an electric bike to get around on? Of course, because that breeds independence. Do I treat people with care and listen to them and try to understand where they are coming from? Of course, because I want to teach my child to be empathetic by showing that I possess that trait, too. Do I continue to learn and try new things? Sure, because I want to show my child that I love learning, too. I cannot stress how much this has helped my parenting, and that's why it is my first point and the best nugget of parenting advice that I have. I have peaked early, so manage your expectations of the rest of the book.

Having a mission statement allows you to make quick decisions. If the answer to a question aids your mission statement, then it's worth pursuing. It focuses your parenting and gives it a long-term goal which makes parenting a lot easier.

Independence

Well, independence is part of the mission statement, so it must be important to me. Isn't the end goal of raising a child to aid in developing an independent person, able to navigate the world, make good and bad decisions and learn from them? The popular term for it is 'grit'.

It saddens me when I see what I call 'wing-clippers'. These are parents who, for many reasons, sometimes unconsciously make sure their children are co-dependent. The ugliest reasons are fear and for their ego. It comes in so many forms: gaslighting, doing all their chores, preparing all their meals, doing all their washing, taking them to and from all their activities and breeding fear.

A child must be able to take care of themselves. Montessori learning focuses on this in the early learning phase where children are responsible for their tasks, washing up after themselves and contributing to the class. Sure, if you let them wash the dishes when they are young, you might have to wash the dishes again after them while they're learning, and it is going to take longer. I remember waiting for my son to get dressed before school, and it took ages. I would internally get impatient. I knew that I could take the jumper and have it on the right way in a tenth of the time. These tasks, as trivial as they seem, help the child learn skills, feel proud and feel like they are contributing to the house ('village') at an early age, and in turn improve their self-esteem. It's a no-brainer: do not be a helicopter parent. It's not love – it's co-dependency, and you are not preparing them to be independent.

There is a fascinating study called the Harvard study of adult development, a longitudinal study that's been going for more than 75 years. It concluded that children who do chores are more successful as adults. They are successful because they gained a work ethic by doing chores at home, according to the analysis.*

* https://www.psychologytoday.com/au/blog/singletons/202211/best-age-kids-start-doing-chores

If they are crying, they are trying to tell you something

Babies are born underdeveloped and are such tender, dependent little people who don't know where they are. The womb sounds like a nice place to hang out, and birthing is tough for all involved, so no wonder babies tend to cry at birth. They have been in the womb for around 9 months and are ejected into a cold world; their eyesight is poor, they are breathing oxygen for the first time, ambient temperatures are fluctuating and, after being inside their mother with continuous contact, they are now free. With all these dramatic changes at birth, it is reasonable to conclude that the infant will want touch, warmth, sleep and food. Save for health issues, which it pains me to think about, if your baby is crying, it's generally one of these 4 basic needs you must fulfil.

Even I can get so testy when I haven't slept. Being a baby who hasn't learned to regulate emotions, it must be a nightmare to be tired. Whenever you can, you should give them the opportunity to sleep. It does make life restrictive, because you owe it to them to give them time to sleep. Sure, you can manipulate the times as they are growing, but babies are all unique. I had friends whose kids would rise at 6 a.m. no matter what time they went to sleep – yawn! How boring. My son as a toddler would sleep eleven hours from when he went to bed. He's developed into a bit of a night owl who loves to sleep in, but I am not overly confident that I had much to do with that. When I pushed the envelope and let him stay up later at family occasions, there was always the increased chance of a tantrum. (I touch on tantrums later.)

I find the concept of controlled crying horrific, where kids are left to 'cry it out' until they fall asleep on their own. The sleeping part of parenting for me was easy as I always laid with my son till he slept, and I generally fell asleep, too. I was a single parent, so it never interrupted sexy time (yes, I just called it sexy time). But if you can't manage to put a child to sleep and save sexy time for another time, then you're doing it wrong.

I can't remember at what age my son stopped afternoon naps, but I can tell you that when we lay down to have those, I often had a second sleep, too. It's a common issue I hear with new parents: they don't get enough sleep. Babies sleep most of the day, so just go to sleep with them and have an afternoon nap. In the end, they will sleep more than you, and you'll have time to do your chores, take a break or catch up on sexy time. (Ok, I won't use that term again!)

My point about controlled crying is that it's used as a tool to aid in regulating sleep patterns, but how can you expect a child to be comfortable being left alone after being so connected for so long? You can paint the walls any colour you like and hang the latest rotating mobile above their bed, but nothing is going to compensate for the touch and security they so desire in this new world.

My son co-slept with me till his teens – not always, but mainly. We still sometimes co-sleep when we travel, and I love it. I believe it aided in our connection.

Touch was not restricted to when we slept. I'm a strong guy and never used a pram, carrying him everywhere instead. We were always touching. Even in his baby seat I would reach back and hold hands. Eventually they will want to touch you less, so I make sure I get as much of that touch as I can while it's still on offer. It doesn't happen often anymore, but my son still sometimes holds my hand. I never make a big deal of it, but inside I'm beaming. It is the sweetest thing in the world. He is now taller than me and still holds my hand and, for the record, signs off on our phone conversations when he's amongst his friends with an 'I love you Papa', even at the expense of being teased. I overheard the girls teasing him in the background as he was hanging up and asked him about it later. He says they do tease him, but he doesn't care.

Damn straight, a child wants to be comfortable, either warm or cool. My son was born in October, which is a month into spring in Melbourne, so it made keeping him warm a lot easier, and having summers where he could get around in his nappies with a light top was great. They do love to be wrapped as babies – don't you think that comes from being in the womb? Anyway, no real anecdotes to add here. Just keep 'em cool or warm.

Food, glorious food. How great if you are fortunate enough to breastfeed your child – the human body is so amazing. Not all people can, and big props to you for making the best out of the situation, whether it's formula or relying on milk donations. These little babies are developing and growing at such a rapid rate that they need wholesome food, and I don't think that ever changes. In an Italian family, we honour food and value mealtime; it's just part of the fabric of our home. I've heard that generationally we are growing taller due to good nutrition. You owe it to your child to feed them a healthy diet. This will allow them to be the best that they can be. Start early so they know what a healthy diet is.

Discipline book

I dated the most wonderful girl when my son was still an infant. She was a girl I'd known from high school who I'd always loved. It should have been a fairytale, but it didn't work out. It's not all bad – she is so happily married now with a new daughter in addition to two sons from a previous marriage. She was light, warmth, care and tenderness in a bundle. I was with her whilst talking about having to discipline, and she put me onto a book called The Discipline Book: how to have a better-behaved child from birth to age ten by William and Martha Sears. I have recommended and purchased this book for various people. It has guided my early parenting so much, and I will be forever grateful to it. You really should be reading that book as opposed to this one. I'll sum up what I remember from the book, but I read it about fourteen years ago, so excuse me if I get some of it wrong.

The Sears were big advocates of co-sleeping and always having the door unlocked should the kids be in their own room, the children knowing that the safe haven of their bed was always open to them. They did have a lock on the door for sexy time (sorry).

If you are connected and have trust with your children, you don't have to discipline, because your children become pleasers and want to please you. Doing the wrong thing and displeasing you is the punishment.

I think the title of this book was so cheeky. I was looking for inventive ways to discipline, but what it gave me was a way to not have to discipline my child (much) by being connected.

Talk to them normally

I always assumed, and saw through some tests, that my kid understood so much, even at a young age. I believe kids often understand more than their parents give them credit for, both verbally and non-verbally. I always named items what they were – penises were, well... penises, and never 'doodle', 'wang' or 'willie'. That may also stem from the fact that I love words. I love a word that just fits, or a word that just sounds great like 'chicane', or a word that describes something that you wouldn't have thought of like 'defenestrate' (which is throwing someone out a window – how cool is that word?). So, I always spoke to my child using the right words. The exception was 'shoe shoe', which I understand is Polish for urinating, but that came from his mother's side and stuck.

Did it work? My son can articulate himself so very well. People would often comment on his ability to communicate, so we used to have a little game we'd play. I would say, 'Yes, he has a very good...' and turn to him, and he would say,

'Vocabulary.' It was super cute, and we still laugh about it now.

We have a standardised test in Australia called NAPLAN, and he was ranked in the top one percent of Australia for his vocabulary, so that speaks for itself. More important than the test result is the love of language that he has. I think it was in part due to talking to him like he was a person, giving him space and respecting that he was intelligent. I extended him respect, and in turn he respects himself.

Two-week shelf

'Oh no Papa, don't put it on the two-week shelf!'

After the mission statement advice, this must come in as number two in my gift to parents. Before I explain the 'two-week shelf' (TWS), let me explain that I never wanted my home to be baby-bombed. It's my house, too. Sure, his bedroom was more child-focused, but if you closed his room, there were barely any signs that there was a child in the house. Also, as my child from the age of two was a student at Montessori, I learned at their open day that the kids' tasks at school are called 'jobs'. The kids can select any job they want and even repeat the same job day in and day out. The kicker was that no matter which job they chose, all the jobs were helping their development. After they finished the job, which was presented on a tray, they had to pack the items back onto the tray and return it to its original shelf. This ethos continued when they used kitchen items and ate food at school. Kids are capable of cleaning up after themselves and get better with practice. This is gold – it keeps the house tidy, frees my time and makes them independent (remember independence is part of the mission statement). It was not without some pushback at times, and that is where the TWS was born.

So, when my son was finished playing, or it was time to go, you had to make time to pack up. If there was ever reluctance, I would calmly say, 'That's ok – I will pack it away on the two-week shelf,' and was always met with, 'Oh no Papa, don't put it on the two-week shelf.' We would talk, all very calmly, and give him the options again. It worked so amazingly well, and my house remains tidy to this day. The TWS can be any high shelf – for us it was on top of a large Ikea bookshelf. What is important is that it's high up, but also where they can see it. So, if I had to pack it away, it would be on the TWS for two weeks and he was unable to play with the item.

You need to appreciate that a kid does not really know what two weeks is, but I assure you that it sounds like a long time. The items were never dated, and the TWS shelf was rarely used. On these rare occasions I would wait for my son to ask for the item, whether it was a week or a month or three months. At that point, I would let him know that there was still a week left. For the TWS to work, there must be a little sting.

Montessori

Full credit goes to his mother for introducing me to Montessori. I'd never heard of it. I had heard of Steiner School, but not Montessori. It's the bane of every Montessori parent that these get grouped together – not that Steiner is inferior. It's very different, and only shares the attribute of being alternative to the normal school system. I remember I went on my own to an open day to check out Montessori, with the normal amount of scepticism I have for everything new. It took me no time to work out that it was how I would want to be educated. It's not overly complicated. The main ethos is to teach a child to love learning, and then you can let them go to be self-directed. There are other parts, including independence, community and responsibility, but the 'teaching them a love of learning' component has been phenomenal.

They gave a good example: kids are ready to learn different skills at different times, and public schools do not account for this. You learn the subject when the syllabus dictates. The example they gave us was that you learn your times table in public school in grade 3. Say that you are not ready to learn them at that age, so you start to carry the burden of 'I am not good at maths', and that will stay for all your interactions with maths moving forward. That is a tragedy. The truth is more likely that you were not ready to learn your times tables at that time, but when you are, you will understand it. At my son's grade 6 graduation, I noticed how many of the students were thanking their teacher for guiding them through maths. It just took the right timing, and Montessori allows for this.

They also aim to have the same teacher for a three-year block, so you can appreciate that the teacher really understands the child, sees them and knows how they are developing. We were so lucky to have great teachers over those years. It would have been problematic if we didn't like the teacher, and had to deal with them for that time, but this didn't eventuate, as their staff were vetted and were excellent.

I make a point of trying to appreciate things before they go wrong, and I thank Montessori all the time for the peace that their approach brought to our house, like the organisation of the home, complete with sticky tabs on all the drawers to let him know which clothes go in which drawers when he was sorting his laundry (I could probably take those off now). The main trait I often acknowledge is how self-directed my son is at learning. I never have to push him to do his homework. The opposite is true – I really try to encourage him to get a good sleep, exercise and have time with friends. I have to suggest he stops studying to get enough rest. There is never an argument in regard to a lack of effort in his schooling – he is committed and dedicated of his own volition. I also make a point of always praising him on his effort, as I believe effort is more important than the result. Unfortunately, I think he places too much emphasis on the result, but he's getting better. There have been times when I know he knows all the material, but it's not reflected in a near-perfect score. I don't care, if I know he applied himself and understands. The past years of tests have been training him to be better at approaching tests for his senior years.

I think we look at tests the wrong way – it's more an identification of what you need to work on, rather than a test for competency. I know they may sound the same. But I look at a test like, 'What parts of the subject didn't you understand so well?' Isn't it great that the test made us aware of these areas, and how can we work on these areas to help you be more well-rounded in the subject? It's only a little change in perception, but it helps a lot.

View them as capable

Kids will grow into the space you give them. Mollycoddle them and there is nowhere to grow. Give them space to make choices, do chores and solve problems. I remember once at a café with friends, my son asked where the toilet was. I had no idea and was enjoying the company of my friends, so I told him to work it out and let me know when he came back. He doesn't have to ask me where the toilet is if he's in a new environment. He can work that out himself. Sure, something could have happened on the way to the toilet – something mild or something horrific –but it was very unlikely that anything else apart from him finding and using the toilet was ever going to happen. It's just one example, and you need to understand that kids are capable of so much. Haven't you seen videos of young kids helping their parents in restaurants prepare, cut, process or cook food? Kids in Japan going to the stores to collect groceries and children of metalworkers using a lathe at an early age?

There are so many examples of kids being capable. You just need to give them space to shine. If they shine, they will build the self-esteem, independence and confidence to be their own person and to tackle life's challenges, especially as they become teenagers.

Try making them pay with your money for items at the register and interacting with the cashier, peeling fruits and vegetables, washing dishes, packing away the laundry and unloading the dishwasher. I have the fondest memories of folding sheets with my mother at a young age – I was so delighted to help. They are going to break and drop items, but those items are going to break eventually. They want to participate – let them, and be patient because it is going to take longer, but they will get better at it. Then there will come a time when you return home to a meal prepared for you or the house cleaned.

Listen to good music

Much like words, I just love music. I don't play an instrument but worked at a radio station and record store as a teenager. It was and continues to be such a large part of my life, from listening, collecting, exploring and seeing it played live. I have inspired my son who shares these traits. Just like words and learning, music is not a task, job or chore; it's a passion – a desire to learn, appreciate and grow. What a joy it is.

'Good music' is such an ambiguous term, and what music moves me is not the same as what moves you. I can tell you that 'Baby shark' does not move me. 'Hot potato' by the Wiggles doesn't move me either, so with me as gatekeeper to the music, my son didn't know of these songs' existence. I did buckle and introduce 'Yo Gaba Gaba', because that was cool, and the messages of 'if you try it, you'll like it' resonated with me. He didn't go crazy for it, but there were a couple of months where he was into it. I tried The Muppet Show too, because that is funny stuff and was nostalgic for me, but it didn't gel with him.

We still share music. It's our love language. We go to a lot of concerts. I stay current with new music because I love it.

I know I rebelled in my teenage years and started listening to punk, grunge and indie music. I am not sure where my son can go to rebel, as I still love those genres. Maybe he will get into Christian rock to rebel against me.

Learn a musical instrument

I did give my son the gift of learning an instrument. I read a New Scientist article about the neural pathways formed from beginning an instrument prior to the age of seven. I think the process, patterns, recollection and dedication also helped in his academic schooling. The piano course recommended practising fifteen minutes a day and starting a discipline at an early age.

You can lead a horse to water, but you cannot make it drink. So, I knew that learning an instrument had to be fun and he had to see the value of learning it. At a very early age, way before he started piano, I would mention how piano is the gateway instrument, how wonderful it would be to connect with people around the world whilst travelling with music. How it could be a feasible career or hobby, allowing you to meet interesting people along the way to cement the value of learning an instrument. So, it was up to the horse to take the drink, but I made sure to let the horse know how sweet the water was. Nine years later, he is still attending lessons once a week and playing the piano of his own accord.

There has been a continuous amount of research supporting the learning of a musical instrument. A recent study published in the Journal of the American Academy of Child & Adolescent Psychiatry found evidence to suggest that playing music alters the behaviour-regulating and motor areas of the brain. This study found that music can change the thickness of the cerebral cortex (a good thing). Benefits listed included for behaviour, working memory, attention control, organisation, future planning, and improved confidence, patience and memory.*

In such a fast-paced, instant world, the process of learning piano has taken nearly a decade, and he continues to build on it. People talk about grit; grit is passion and perseverance, and learning an instrument requires that discipline over a long period of time. That lesson alone is enough of a reward from learning an instrument, let alone the ability to play.

* https://www.sciencedaily.com/releases/2014/12/141223132546.htm

Talk about sex

Who said you can't get life advice from Salt'N'Pepa? I think we've all moved away from the stork delivering the baby – well, everyone in my hipster bubble has, anyway. Sex is so important for both reproduction and connection. It's such a drive from the teenage years and onwards. It needs to be addressed openly and honestly. Sure, shape it to their age, but be honest and open if you want them to be honest and open with you when they're older.

I just started with the penis going into the vagina. That was just the beginning. It wasn't long before I got the 'Why?' It wasn't too hard. Firstly, I explained the seed (semen) and the egg, and that it's for reproduction; but I didn't fall short, and I let him know that people mainly do it because it feels good. I think that blew his mind. It's hard to comprehend for a little kid, but gee as they approach ten years of age, they become increasingly fascinated by it.

We are fortunate to have gay and lesbian friends, so that was never awkward. It was just part of the building of his knowledge from me, and not from kids making it up in the playground. We still talk about sex, and I am candid about my own bachelor activity. I don't get into specific detail, but he is aware I have an active sex life. I do think as we approach him becoming sexually active, that he will share with me when he feels the need to. I don't need to know the details, but if he wants any information, he can always ask me or the internet. Come to think of it, he will probably ask the internet first.

Talking about sex freely and early allows you to transition to new topics, such as contraception, sexually transmitted infections and the whole gamut of subsections which arise in this topic. Starting with truth is always the best foundation.

I would class myself as sex positive, so I have really focused on consent, because that is the basis for the start of a healthy sexual interaction. It has become such a hot topic, but my feelings are that whatever floats your boat is up to the people if there's consent. I wish it were that simple – consent is also tricky. You must consider whether the person is rational or inebriated to be able to give that consent.

It is good to be bored

I am a 'doer'. I like to plan events and stay busy, but then I like to just chill out and do my own thing. It's not my job to make sure that my child is always entertained, and I don't mean giving them a screen to fill the void, either. I have let my son know from an early age that if he is bored it's his own fault, as there is so much to play with and explore. I do not think I've ever heard him say, 'I'm bored.' I think screens are useful, but I would suggest that they're a treat, not the norm.

With screens I think it's important to avoid commercials. These are so clever at cultivating want, so I never have the TV playing in the background, and I ensure that most screen time was not on free-to-air TV which is full of commercials. Also, the kid-directed shows and games are so bright, colourful and fast paced that you're going to find the pace of school difficult if you consume a lot of it.

Kids love to play, whether with toys, in sport, at the playground or with each other. Time moves fast, so the preteenager years are a great time to foster this. In households that rely on screens, I equally see a mountain of toys lying idle. Pick a lane, but be careful and don't expect toys to be able to compete with the passive enjoyment of screens.

I am lifting this straight from @raisingwellkids[*] on Instagram. In the space of boredom is where kids develop skills to self-regulate. They find things to do that are steered solely by their self-interests. They have untethered access to their own thoughts, without being influenced by ours. Boredom lets them reach the depths of imagination, and they experiment with creativity. So embrace boredom.

[*] https://www.instagram.com/raisingwellkids/?hl=en

Do not over-consume

This refers to both physically and mentally. Mentally I am talking about the impact of how cluttered our houses have become with toys and items. Physically I am referring to how parents feel the need to prepare food and always feed their children.

Have you ever seen a kid at a birthday party or celebration receive so many gifts that they're just tearing the wrapping off each gift and moving on? How much we consume is a little disgusting.

I once had a girlfriend with whom I spent one Christmas with her family. The mountain of presents – mostly plastic – was a display of their love for their children, which should have been beautiful, but to me was horrendous. They were great people, and the kids were lovely, but there were so many presents. How can you pick what to play with, and how do you value them when there are so many alternatives? It's all a bit weird to me. People bring gifts because they are conditioned to do so. If there are a lot of gifts, try hiding them and bring them out another time. If it's customary to open them, just put them away quickly and drip feed them over the year, re-gift them or donate them. If your child asks for the gift later, you can give it to them, but it's generally 'out of sight and out of mind' with toys.

Mmmm, sugar – it's delicious, void of nutrition and full of energy. If you've never observed how kids respond to sugar like it's crack cocaine, then you need to look harder. That's the alarm bell. I've seen the same reaction of children to chips and ice cream as with addicts and drugs. I've seen videos comparing children's response to sugar to that of the response to cocaine in adults, but these sources were questionable. Just look at kids – the greed and desire that comes from these foods. Now picture them in their teenage years being offered drugs and how their gratification patterns will extend to these items.

Am I meant to offer a solution now? I'm not sure I have one. We have succumbed to the delights of sugar. I would make sure when we flew in planes that we had lollipops to help with the equalising of the air pressure. Now that is a solid little travel tip. We love desserts, and gelati is one of my favourite foods. Having said this, for your own health and the health of your children, you must manage the intake. Chips (crisps) are not for daily consumption; lollies are not daily, either. Vegetables – plain, steamed, roasted or with a sauce – are delicious. It's always a good idea to start your meal with a salad. You owe it to yourself and your children.

You are shaping their future eating habits, so practise what you preach. I don't want to fat-shame, but being obese is damaging to your health; and if you see an obese child, they are commonly accompanied by obese parents, so this behaviour is often learnt. I hear comments like 'fast food is cheaper', 'sugary food is cheap and tempting'. Try going to a market – I think they are so much fun to go to. I am the worst haggler. I try, but I always pay the ticketed price. In contrast to my haggling techniques, I am a little savvy, and I tend to go mid-afternoon to a cheaper market in my area where I can get end-of-day deals. I can make a ratatouille for about $25 to serve about 15 meals of vegetable goodness. You can get end-of-day deals on fish, meat and veggies. It just takes some planning and leveraging off seasonal foods, which are cheaper. On occasion, I buy frozen salmon which is so easy to prepare, and delicious. I am not a nutritionist and have struggled with fluctuating weight my whole life. Should we ever meet, be prepared to not see the sculpted Adonis I am presenting myself as, but I am healthy.

I have heard advice to stick to the outer aisles of the supermarket for better eating, and it is solid advice. Sure, the middle has some necessities, but the main shopping should come from the outer fruit and vegetable, dairy and frozen areas. I have noticed since making a conscious decision to eat better that when I arrive home, most of my shopping needs to be refrigerated.

Do not wait for them

Maybe this comes from ego, which I'm not proud of, but when we went for walks or outings I would rarely if ever wait for my son. I would just walk. If he was distracted, I might wait if it was interesting or deserved some exploration. Otherwise, I'd just walk, and it was up to him to keep up. Same happened while shopping. I would just move to the next aisle. I was always amazed at how I could hear my son's voice in a noisy room – it was some Steve Austin super-hearing stuff going on. It's a bit harsh, but I think that most toddlers are sociopaths, and they're trying to manoeuvre and construct a world where their needs are met with minimal effort and no consideration for others.

If there was ever a time to teach them who the boss is, it's in these years. Buckling to all their whims and desires and giving them what they want when they ask for it are such bad habits. These little people just do not have the mechanisms for complex decision-making. They're not empathetic at an early age, and empathy is one of the parts of the mission statement. So now is your time to work on this before it's too late.

Let them lead

I guess what I am trying to say in these last two chapters can be better summed up in a great video I saw of Doctor Garor Maté who amongst other qualifications is an author and physician with a special interest in childhood development. He talks about the three modes of parenting: permissive, authoritative and authoritarian, which was originally identified by a 1960s psychologist Diana Baumrind. The permissive parent allows all behaviour and doesn't intervene; he advises against this mode and says it is the worst thing you can do, advising that parenting is not a democracy, it is a hierarchy. For the authoritative parent, although sounding harsh, the aim is not to dominate, suppress or exploit the child, but to nurture and support, teaching the child to handle responsibility, overcome difficulties and be confident in their own judgement. Finally, the authoritarian parent is based on strict rules with no room for interpretation, compromise or discussion. This can lead to a 'follower' mentality and low self-esteem.

So, when I say don't wait for them, let them know that you are the leader and you determine the rules and what is going to happen; and when I say let them lead, allow them to explore, and support and nurture them.

You are the priority

Sure, I love my son more than I love myself. I really would sacrifice a lot for him, even my life. But I am the priority. We are all important, but I must prioritise my wellbeing and self-care so I can be a better parent to my child. I think my child would want this, too. There is no chasm between their care and mine, as they are interrelated. If I stay physically and mentally happy, then my child will benefit, so it's like a circle of awesomeness.

Throughout my parenting, I have ensured I have self-cared by maintaining strong friendships, watching my diet, having my own personal goals and playing sports. I have even travelled without my son, although I do love travelling with him. I need to fill my cup so I am happy. Kids see so much and they can read the room better than most adults give them credit for. So, if there is a piece missing from the parent, they can see it. So take care of yourself and you will all benefit from it.

There is a wonderful speech by Tich Nhat Hanh, a great Buddhist teacher, which is easy to find on YouTube. He says,

'The greatest gift a parent can give to their child is their own happiness. Parents don't have to leave behind a huge sum of money in order for their children to be happy.' This is what I mean by 'You are the priority'.

‘That's what my parents did’ is the worst reason to keep on doing it

I’ve heard this term come out of a few people’s mouths as justification for bad parenting. I really am thinking about one friend, but if you know me, you know who I’m thinking of, and we all know I can’t use his name... It’s Jason. He is a real champ, good guy and family man. I’ve known him since high school, and I’ve heard this phrase come from his mouth more often than any other person’s. Growing up, he didn’t have the healthiest of family relationships, and he will continue to parrot the advice and mimic the actions of his parents, believing they are correct. You must have a growth mindset to continually change – that’s part of my self-care routine. You must evaluate what happened, consider it in the context of the times, and change to include what we know today.

My parents are wonderful people. My mother passed away at a young age. She was a lovely, caring mother, but with my adult eyes I see that she was a racist who was not overly informed from growing up on a tiny, isolated island. I would like to think she would have grown to change. But it does seem that as people get older, they become more rigid. My father, who has grown to be a recycler and a supporter of the gay marriage vote, still drops some questionable comments from time to time. He is currently eighty-eight and not as open to change, and is reverting to his beliefs he created when he was a young man in Italy.

I hope that practices like controlled crying will become a thing of the past, just like spanking. I caught a late-night documentary about twenty years ago about a scientist named Harry Harlow who experimented on monkeys in the 1950s and 1960s. He really did put them in awful situations, and as his experiments progressed, they became more and more controversial. He did not hide that fact, with experiment titles such as 'Rape rack' and 'Pit of despair', both of which I will refrain from explaining due to their brutality. Harlow received protests and eventually his work was halted, but his work changed parenting for the better.

One of his early experiments was the 'Monkey mother', where newborn monkeys were taken from their mothers and placed in a cage with a steel wire surrogate with fabric around it. He altered this experiment by having the same fabric monkey beside a completely wire monkey with food, and the baby monkeys would hold on to the fabric monkey and reach for the food.

Prior to these experiments it was thought in the Western world that a mother's love was dangerous and would lead to adult issues in a child. We've heard the term 'mummy's boy': boys were told to 'be boys', and fathers were a lot more distant emotionally. It's through Harlow's research that the importance of touch and affection to the development of children began to be recognised.

I see fathers today and they have really stepped up, taking more responsibility. I think there has been a major shift in parenting, and it's exciting that it's evolving. So don't do it just because your parents did it.

Nudity

We have a national radio station in Australia called Triple J, and they had a talkback section where they were discussing at what age you should stop being naked in front of your children. There was a different answer from each person based on their upbringing. The most interesting call came from a girl who was dating a boy from one of the Nordic countries – it may have been Sweden. She told a story about how the previous year, she went there for Christmas and enjoyed a lunch with her boyfriend's parents and his siblings. Following the meal, the family proceeded to get naked and hop in the sauna together. It was a difficult experience for her, but I just love that story, because the answer is that tolerance of nudity is a social construct. There is no right answer.

I was always weirded out by the dude that likes to get naked at parties and run around inebriated, and I am by no means a nudist in public. But I made a point of not being ashamed of being nude in my household, and I want to encourage body positivity. I am still nude in the house, but it's mainly from the shower to the bedroom or something like that. My son who is well into puberty also will go from room to room naked. I really like this – I want him to be comfortable in his body. I have spoken to friends about this, and the best question I received was, 'Do you think it would be different if my son was a daughter?' We will never know, but yes, that may have changed the nude dynamic. I just think the human body is beautiful, and with all the hang-ups in a modern world, we don't need any more.

A deal is a deal

I was fortunate to be brought up in a trusting family. Even my brothers are reliable and caring, and they have integrity. We are all businessmen. Between us we have seven children, and two of us have grandchildren. They are all solid, interesting and good kids. I am really amazed and grateful for how devoid of problems our family has been to this point.

Perhaps it is this family trait with a penchant for business that cemented that 'A deal is a deal'. It sounds simple, and it's something I've always said to my son. I would start the sentence with, 'A deal is a...' and he would respond with, 'Deal'. Sure, a cat is a cat; a banana is a banana. But 'a deal is a deal' is so much more. I think there are so many lessons here. It makes us responsible for our agreements and fosters integrity. A deal can be broken with a mutual agreement. Due to its importance, my son would consider the deal and its ramifications prior to agreeing, and if he thought the deal too difficult to honour, he would refuse or ask to alter the deal. Great lessons there in consideration, trust, honour, integrity, negotiation and planning, all bundled into one little sentence.

Paul E Di Cintio

You are not their friend

My son and I joke around a lot, even haze each other. It's a fine line to dance. I noticed that it's a habit of our family to challenge the younger kids with teasing – nothing too bad. But it is a strange habit which requires delicacy, and which I don't necessarily recommend. I considered this practice and understood that it's a character-building exercise, where you place the kid in a difficult situation and they have to use their wits to navigate it. It's very tricky, but I think it does have benefits.

On a recent holiday I had to pull my son up about the way he was talking to me, as the hazing was getting a little sharp. He said, 'I thought we are friends?' I was taken aback and asked for some time to think about his question. I came back and let him know that we are most certainly not friends. Friends come and go, and friends care, but what we have is so much more. I will always be there for him, love him more than anything else. I am devoted and focused on him being the best person he can be. Calling us 'friends' really undersells our relationship. Consequently, I deserve acknowledgement and respect for the commitment I have to his rearing. I know they say you're meant to give without expecting anything in return, but I want love, respect, and acknowledgement for the effort I put in. I get so much in return – I really am a better person for being a parent, so I am forever grateful to him – but I do expect the gratitude to be reciprocated.

I recently came across Michelle Obama talking about the very same topic, and she advises against being your child's friend. A friend is someone who you like and want to be liked by. A parent must educate, lead and discipline amongst other things, and you just can't be concerned as to whether your child likes you, 'cause at times they will not.

I also saw a Jordan Peterson speech which I thought was special. He spoke about kids being one hundred percent on board with having the best relationship with you, more than anyone else in your life; that means that you could have a better relationship with your child than with anyone. That is what they offer you, and that is the best opportunity. But remember, you are more than their friend.

Jokes are important

The nuances of jokes and wordplay are amazing. It takes a lot of processing and sophistication to interpret and understand the wordplay or the situation – to get the joke. What a wonderful thing it is for a kid when the penny drops. This happens when you look back at an event through a more mature window to better interpret the situation; it often happens with jokes. I would tell the joke, 'My dog has no nose.' My son knew how to respond: 'How does it smell?' I would respond with, 'Terrible!' and begin laughing, and he wouldn't get it. I love that joke. It still makes me laugh, and I have told it too many times to count. I remember my son when he returned from school one day to let me know when the penny dropped.

We enjoy comedy to this day, with our favourite comedians being Ricky Gervais and Bill Burr. These comedians give us a new, challenging way to look at the world. Challenging our norms and beliefs, they really provide a community service. We also like Jimmy Carr. He's so witty, sharp and inappropriate. I always wanted to thank Jimmy for 8 out of 10 Cats Does Countdown, that show we discovered during lockdown and which really helped us get through it. It combines some of our favourite things: word play, mathematics and humour.

You are flawed, it's OK

Oh, my goodness – I am so flawed. You hear the stories of kids when they are in their teens having the veil lifted and seeing their parents, with all their foibles, falling off the pedestal. Sure, it might feel good to be on the pedestal as a parent, but you are bound to fall off. I think it's important to let kids know that you are flawed and make many mistakes and will continue to do so. I think it helps them make mistakes and lets them know that you are still growing and changing, and the same is true for them now and for the future. I do love the idea of a growth mindset, and admitting you are flawed allows for being open to change and growth.

It also allows you to change your mind. If you act in an inappropriate way and realise it later, you can apologise and talk about the error you made. You need not be so rigid as to stick to your first reaction. I think that is a good lesson, too.

I could equally write a book called 'Parents are dicks' and list all the things I have done wrong; it would be a bigger book than this one.

Be the shepherd

This I saw on an Instagram reel. It was from a talk by Dr Barkley, and I thought it was brilliant. He talks about a child being born with four hundred traits which are a mosaic of your parents' genetic backgrounds. It really adds weight to choosing the right partner to procreate with. He goes on to say that parents these days have more guilt than ever, believing they have ownership over the child and that the child's successes are the parent's successes; and concurrently, their failures are the parent's failures, too. I think this is a bit narrow, as poor parenting can really affect those traits too, but the essence of what he's saying is remarkable. He suggests that rather than ownership, the parent should take the role of a shepherd: providing a safe space for the child to grow, ensuring they are safe, warm and secure, and fending off danger, but letting them roam. He adds that the role of the shepherd is important, and you should be proud of that role.

I really like this viewpoint. I have given my son such a strong upbringing, and what he chooses to do with that is up to him. I have let him know this. It removes my responsibility, but importantly, makes him responsible for his own future – to make good decisions for his benefit or detriment. I will always be there to help him and guide him, but they are his decisions.

You can't always get what you want

It is such a life truth, so why not prepare them early? There was never a separate meal prepared just for my child. He ate what was on the table. He did not rule the house. I was the boss and decided what we were doing. Sure, he had input, but kids are not sophisticated enough to make these decisions. Ask a kid what they want for dinner and you might hear something like ice cream or chocolate. If this is not a red flag for how naïve they are, I don't know what is. So, understand that they are not the decision makers because they are not sophisticated enough, and it will save you a lot of pain.

This also leads to delayed gratification. I read that instant gratification is stronger in boys than with girls and made a point to offer a little now and more later to train this desire for gratification. There is a famous 'marshmallow test' showing kids struggling with instant gratification – you can google this. I think instant gratification may coincide with drug use later in life. There are many other factors to that, but knowing my own history, I have been conscious of shaping my son's behaviour to minimise this. If I am just the shepherd, then it has all been in vain and he will be what he can be, but I do think that these are the little training moments to help foster the good traits.

Do not watch commercial television

Full disclosure here: my career has been mainly in the production of TV commercials. They are awful, sophisticated things whose main objective is to breed want. That is a little brutal, as some are informative and change bad attitudes. There is some good in there, but you cannot filter the TV commercials – they are just presented to you. Kids' television is the worst, with brightly coloured and smiley commercials. If you want to watch something, I think you should avoid commercial television and even YouTube, so you can shelter them from this.

Do not compare against other kids

I had a friend who was an early learning teacher. He was a good source of child anecdotes. Prior to becoming a parent, I remember he would let me know about conversations with parents where they would praise the strength of their child. Let's use mathematics for this example: his inner monologue was something to the effect of, 'Sure he's great at maths, but he is socially inept.' My friend was brutal. His point was that parents compare traits and skills amongst kids; it's hard not to do. What my friend told me was that kids develop at different rates in different areas, but by the time they reach eleven they tend to balance out. There are developmental issues you need to look out for – you would hope that parents and teachers should identify these – but outside of this, just know that it's going to be all right in the end. Sure, Alfred can read by the age of five, and that is his strong skill; but Bruce will get there too in his own time. At eleven, Alfred may still be a better reader, but Bruce will be able to read too, and Bruce might be better than Alfred as a mathematician, socialiser, parkour athlete or macramé practitioner.

Parents will tend to spew their child's most advanced features, so do not worry if your child is not there yet. There is plenty of time for that developmental measure, and they will likely get there. Love them and yourself for the developing, learning wonderful people that you and they are.

Delayed gratification

I want it I want it I want it! Yuck – a child protesting for something of insignificance is awful, and if they do it a lot it's because it's worked in the past. My least favourite subject is talking about Covid and the lockdowns, so I promise I won't labour on it. One of the first items to be cleared from stores was toilet paper. Seriously – people were fighting over it. I heard a psychologist explain that the population, whose only skill is consuming, went into a frenzy, and to feel secure did the only thing that they were capable of: consume. I found this so sad, and it makes me reflect on how we function in the Western world. I am not averse to having items of beauty or convenience, but I find over-consumption disgusting. Did I digress? Probably. Will I do it again? Most definitely.

So, there must be tools to ensure that the child must work for, earn or simply not get everything they want. Simply saying 'ask me in an hour' will result in the child forgetting. Whatever want they felt at the time will fade. Not a bad rule to have for yourself when it comes to internet shopping, too.

If you buckle when they are having a tantrum and give in to the tantrum, rest assured that you will get more tantrums because your child has worked out that they are a successful course of action.

You are part of a team

We have spent a lot of time in Bali, and I have also spent some time in India. Both places, aside from being predominantly Hindu, have the happiest people I have encountered. Sure, Bali is a lush paradise, but India has a much harsher environment. I have often considered why they are so happy, and to me it has come down to one common attribute: village living. The Harvard longitudinal study I mentioned earlier also confirms this.

How rich are these children's lives – they can gain knowledge from many sources, are loved and cared for by many people and share stories with the young and old. Western life lacks this attribute. It's such an isolated life, and the density of the modern city seems to be inversely proportional to a sense of community. I do see elements of a strong community in the country and certain suburbs, but it is far from village-style living.

Contributing or being part of a team helps with self-esteem. Your life extends outside of yourself, and people depend on you, so you become responsible. The same goes for the home. If the child does not contribute by keeping their room clean, putting away their clothes, doing dishes or making their bed, it's just time taken away from the parent connecting with the child. Make sure the child knows the household requires a team effort to make it work. Encourage your child to see how other families work and have influences from outside of the immediate family.

The only child needs to learn to forgive

This is through my own observation, but I think that having siblings helps immensely in conflict resolution. Sure, they fight and argue, but they learn to forgive and move on. It really is a gift to prepare them for relationships in the future. I noticed that my son, being an only child, takes conflict more seriously and with less forgiveness. The conflict is spoken about as a terminal event. I am not sure of the solution. I know I try to lead and say sorry a lot and try to forgive easily.

My son did have a nemesis in primary school. They were combative, and I did point out that they were similar people and that one day they might be good friends. That boy moved internationally in high school, but not before they started spending time together and hanging out. Let kids know that conflict is setting boundaries, and just because they have set a new boundary or it has been crossed, doesn't mean that it's a final event.

Kids need to tussle

We've all seen tiger cubs and puppies wrestle. I'm not saying wrestle with your child if they don't instigate it, but a lot of kids love that kind of play. Sometimes they don't know when to stop, or they go too far, but this along with the release of energy are all part of the lesson. It will help them to know what is appropriate if they ever tussle outside of the home.

There is a great article on the National Childbirth Trust website* about oxytocin, your happy hormone. This hormone is released when children interact with their parents. Interestingly though, the activity that produces the most oxytocin for parent and child differs depending on whether the child is interacting with their mum or dad.

In dad's case, and probably why I advocate the need to tussle, the father and his child get a peak in oxytocin from playing with each other. This is why dads can seem to prefer

* https://www.nct.org.uk/

playing to caretaking, and children preferentially seek them out as play partners. So while dad is sometimes labelled as the 'fun' parent, there is a real reason behind his desire to play with his children.

This is not to say that dads don't get a neurochemical reward from caring for their baby. It's just not quite as big a hit as a good bout of rough-and-tumble play.

You can make it somewhere on your own

I have already touched on the Japanese who send their kids on errands on their own. I am not proposing this at such an early age in the Western world. Japan is different, where there is a community who supports this activity, but you can start small. Put the bins out, walk to a friend's house. Complete practice runs together, but then let them try on their own. Talk to them about what to do if they get lost – who would be best to speak to? My son started catching the tram to school in grade 5. We did a practice run together, but the first time he did it on his own he got off the tram about one kilometre too early. He called me to let me know, and he was a little concerned that he was running late. I told him not to worry and to make his way casually to school; arriving at school a little late was going to be fine. I did speak to his teacher about this at a later parent-teacher interview, and the teacher was delighted that my son had made a mistake, having to solve a problem and be independent, mentioning that these are the important parts of schooling. The teacher noted that he will likely never take the wrong stop again, and he never did.

Fear is the development killer

Please be careful what news sources you consume. We have commercial TV stations, and they impart fear to get higher ratings: 'Home invasions and gang violence among other threats are right outside on the street and in your homes.' I know that there are versions of this in most countries. I live in Melbourne, Australia, in a leafy, inner-city town called Elwood. It is so pretty and adjacent to St Kilda, which is still pretty but has a seedier edge, though it's no Compton, Los Angeles (apologies if you are from Compton – I have never been there, but it's the first place which came to mind). Times have never been statistically safer, but talking to people who live in fear, you would think otherwise.

I remember as a kid riding around the neighbourhood with freedom to explore, normally with a friend or in packs. Our parents didn't know where we were for most of the day. 'At home for dinner or before sunset' was the standard curfew. These days, parents are ferrying their children to and from events and playdates. The kids are unable to make it there on their own. What a missed opportunity for growing resilience and fostering adventure and independence.

I think the greatest risk my child undertakes is riding his bike. He travels around five kilometres to school, even more when there are piano lessons or tennis lessons after school. But risks are just that, and they're everywhere. You just can't remove them – you can only mitigate them. I've spent time driving around with my son and talking about potential risks when on the road, which is a good lesson for riding, and for the future when he starts driving. I see the risk, mitigate the risk, and either accept or reject the risk. The thought that something could happen is awful, but I can't protect him from these unlikely occurrences when he's on his own. I feel the same about surfing. People ask, 'What about the sharks?' Seriously, that is so unlikely that it's not worthy of factoring. Do I kick my legs up in the air if I catch a shadow in the water? Sure, but it is not going to stop me, because it just doesn't add up. Protecting your child from all risk is impossible, and trying to doesn't arm them with the skills to tackle challenges later in life.

As I'm writing this section, I've just spoken to my son about a white-water rafting school camp he's just returned from. We've been on some adventure tours, been kayaking and hiking, so he does have experience in these areas. He was telling me about the camp, and I was filled with joy. It was difficult and challenging for him, but he maintained a great attitude. He helped kids who were feeling negative about the experience or got sick and exhausted. During one of our hikes, which is a great place to share stories, I had explained the idea of 'future fun', so he was armed with that knowledge and experience: he has embarked upon these types of challenges before and loved them. During this school camp he shared the concept of future fun with his friends and teachers to help them.

Future fun? Say what? Don't google it, because it doesn't exist. It was introduced to me by a learned and articulate friend, but I think he pinched it from somewhere else. It's when you are undertaking a challenge like camping, hiking or most other adventurous activities. At times they seem difficult or daunting, but you must remember that when you look back on it in the future, you will have a story. You will invariably look upon it favourably and with gratitude. That is 'future fun'.

Being sick is boring

I am not the best person to be sick around, and I am not the best person when I'm sick. I'm not talking about serious illness – I'm talking about 'colds, flus and aches' types of sickness. I am also not talking about mental illness, which requires care. I hope that your life is devoid of both minor and major illnesses.

I just want to get back on the horse and keep riding. I will work through minor illnesses and rest as I have to, but I don't like to stop because of illness. It's also a sad topic to talk about and should be avoided everywhere. Sure, there are instances when stories of illness serve as a warning or advice, but they are dull and on occasion are there to evoke sympathy. I am so sorry you have been mildly sick, but I do not want to talk about it.

I think this rigid viewpoint comes from a combination of rarely being home from school for being sick, because my parents were not cut that way, and losing my mother to cancer at an early age. Sure, my son has stayed home because of illness, but I don't make it a fun time – minimise the delay and move on. I think that the lack of being allowed to stay home from school by my parents helped with building my strong work ethic. I also think it's dangerous to give children especially good treatment when they're sick. I'm not saying don't take care of them – I feel I am balancing on a very thin ledge right now – I'm saying do not create a better environment and reinforce that being sick is a rewarding thing. I think it can become a treat to be sick. So, if they aren't getting much attention at home, or school is difficult, they may use sickness to avoid it. I would much rather take a day off school to do something great than mask it to avoid an issue with illness.

Love learning

I think a love of learning is innate. From the moment we are born we are developing – also known as learning. If a child is engaged, you can just leave them to it. There are many simple tasks that help a child: pouring and separating help with motor skills, for example. Moving around helps with coordination; grocery shopping helps with mathematics, nutrition, values, society norms, buyer behaviour and interactions. I once read that your child will learn more from grocery shopping than visiting an art gallery. I am not super fond of this, but they might be right in the short term. But making your child appreciate beauty and art will also help long term.

As mentioned, a cornerstone of Montessori education is fostering a love of learning. I think the key is what I touched on in the last paragraph: engagement. Don't worry about what the subject matter is – they will build on it later if they're engaged in whatever they're doing. It will keep them wanting more.

Ditch the pram

Ditch the pram, ditch the snacks, and maybe keep a drink. For newborns sure, you need nappies, wipes and all the other stuff I can't remember. But keep it light – make life easy for you. Your child will want to be attached to you. I'm strong so I could manage to carry my child everywhere. If I was not, I could have bought a sling. I love those slings. It's so close to being in the womb for the child.

Healthy eating advice seems to change every six months; however, the Mediterranean diet seems to remain a constant. It includes meals at mealtimes. Your child is not going to be malnourished if they don't have a snack between meals. I'm not sure if they even value it, and it's generally suggested by the parent. So, make your life easier: organise main meals and ditch the unnecessary.

One meal for the whole family

The idea that I would prepare more than one meal is preposterous, save for any dietary requirements. What is on the table is on the table. This is not an à la carte restaurant. Food has been considered, purchased and prepared for your nourishment, and with love too, so be grateful and eat it. If you aren't hungry that's fine, but there is no other meal between now and the next meal.

I know the above may sound harsh to some, but I love feeding my son, and he always loved trying new things. A love of food seems to be a family trait – our extended family meals, orchestrated by Joe, my brother who is a chef, are so remarkable that a similar food experience is almost impossible to find. My son never goes hungry, and I do cater to our tastes to make mealtime appealing.

I remember giving my son an analogy: if he spent an hour painting a picture, I would ensure I gave it some attention and appreciated it. The same goes for a meal. Some pictures are better than others, but you have to appreciate the effort which has gone into it, too.

Children are really interested in growing bigger and taller. I really drove this and always associated that a broad range of foods would help supply the necessary nutrition to help the body grow to its full potential. The generations get taller because of better nutrition, so it's obvious. Failing to get the right nutrition at the right time can affect development. So let your child know that their choices significantly impact their development, and make them appreciate the taste and value of food.

Three things you do not have to eat

You eat what's been served, but I'm not an arsehole. I had a deal (and now you know how important a deal is in my family) with my son: he could pick three ingredients he didn't have to eat. He could change these ingredients, but not without waiting twenty-four hours for the change to come into effect. We would write the list on the fridge, but in truth we barely used the list, and I think beans may have been there once along with asparagus, but I can't remember what else. He does eat both of those now.

We all have different tastes, so you shouldn't have to eat something you really don't like. You want to avoid kids becoming fussy, so expose them to a variety of flavours early. If you aren't careful, they will only want to eat fruit and chocolate, and that is not enough nutrition.

Honesty

In my mid-twenties I dated a girl and just loved her family as much as I loved her. Her father, Raymond, was such a great influence in my life, and we spoke honestly and candidly about life. I wouldn't have said I was a dishonest person prior to that – I had done some mildly questionable things – but I remember him saying that honesty was a cornerstone of his family. I have really taken this on in every part of my life. Honesty can be challenging with a child. There are some questions which make you pause, like, 'What is a condom?' followed by, 'Why didn't you use one with my mother?' which was a doozy. 'Why do you not like my mother?' That was a challenge. But I tried to shape the answers to his age, and always responded with honesty.

The question from my son I remember most was, 'What is (the drug) ecstasy like?' I paused for a moment longer than usual having been put on the spot, the various answers I could give running through my head, and my response was... 'It's wonderful.' He stared at me in astonishment and silence. After a long pause I launched into how ecstasy works by releasing serotonin, and you feel connected to the world and people, but it drains the serotonin and makes you feel down in the coming days; and that it's not for everyone, but I think everyone should try it. Tough question, but for me an honest answer. My son looked up at me at the end of the discussion and thanked me for being so honest with him. It was a proud moment, but I'm still concerned I have yet to realise the consequence of my honesty from that day. I reiterated that story to a friend who thinks I am totally irresponsible. He may be right. I probably should have left this anecdote out of the book.

Sociopath

A close friend would refer to toddlers as sociopaths. I don't think he was too far off. Rather than a mental condition, it seems that a lot of toddlers are not interested in others' feelings and are just directed to fill their food and entertainment desires with no regard for anyone else. Like I mentioned, they are not sophisticated enough to make good decisions at an early age, and fostering this unempathetic behaviour will result in poor self-control and a lack of empathy. Do not give them whatever they want, but explain why, and remember: you are the boss.

Other kids are dicks

They really are dicks. And be confident that our kids, even if they are nice at home, can be dicks outside of the house. So many stories from the schoolyard reinforce that kids can be awfully rude and manipulative. I'm not trying to totally minimise their opinions and actions, but I just think it's important to let your child know that what other kids say and do can be meaningless, naïve or without constructive intentions, and that you should judge for yourself. Looking outwardly for reinforcement is dangerous, and leads to everyone being the same, which is totally boring and rarely a good measure.

I think this mantra has helped minimise the impact of any bullying and issues that have arisen from interactions with other children. I am also concerned that my son often feels more mature than other children and can inadvertently ostracise himself from his friendship group. For inner-city living, his school only has eight kids in year 11 next year, so the pool of children to engage with has been small, and ostracising yourself can cause isolation. The benefits of his education are that his teachers are so engaged and understand my child so well. I don't think he's met his tribe as yet, but I know that will come and hope that that tribe is a good bunch.

I get the window seat

I might not get the mango cheek, but I always get the window seat. We have a saying in our home: 'You always get the mango cheek.' I used to comment that since having a child, whenever we eat a mango, I'm left with the pip. In essence, he always gets the best part. I was maybe overly sensitive to my son showing signs of greed when he was younger. I really think it's improved with time. The truth was that when I was serving ice cream, cutting a cake, distributing chocolate or pouring a drink, he would always get the best part, but he was looking and analysing the whole time. I banned my least favourite four-letter 'f' word from our household: 'fair', because when he was younger, he didn't understand what fair meant – or rather, he had a strong sense of what he thought it meant. It only meant from his point of view, he wasn't getting what he thought he deserved, and he was too basic to understand the complexities of fairness, so I didn't allow him to use it in the house. It worked. I don't know how enforceable it was, but it worked. Kids don't understand 'fair', so let them know that their developing brains cannot comprehend what it means. I cringe whenever a child uses that word.

He did taunt me with the word 'fair', saying it repeatedly if he was angry, but I was laughing on the inside knowing how supple this word was compared to other four-letter words.

What was the part about the window seat? We have flown together many times and only on a couple of occasions has he had the window seat. I'm bigger, I paid for it, and I should get it. There is no question about it. It just makes sense that the little person should be between to larger adults for comfort. Let them know that your wellbeing and desires are important too, and that they don't always get the mango cheek.

Grocery shopping is fun

I enjoy grocery shopping, supermarkets and markets. I even enjoy visiting them internationally to see the variety of items they sell. It's an opportune time to discuss nutrition, pricing and how corporate manipulation influences buying. Planning, preparing for meals, saving money, trying new items and haggling at the market are all important skills to develop. It's also one-on-one time. Sure, I didn't use a pram, but I did use a trolley when completing large shops at the supermarket. Kids are right there looking at you, assessing you and the world around them. It's a great time to connect, learn and have fun.

You have already won the lottery

I love coming across videos of Neil deGrasse Tyson. The gist of one of his stories was how people say, 'If only I won the lottery, oh what I would do!' The likelihood that you as this person, made up of stardust and conceived at that specific moment, with that specific sperm and egg, to make it through childbirth to become this specific person, is statistically mind-blowing. He talks about how precious your life is: of the one hundred billion people who have ever lived, out of the more than quadrillions of genetic combinations, it is so statistically unlikely that you would have been born to experience the beauty of the world. On top of that, if you were born into the Western world, which is the safest it has ever been, then guess what? You've already won the lottery, because the chances of winning the lottery are small, but to have had all those factors occur is even smaller. So, take advantage of it, and make the most of the winning the greatest lottery of them all.

Racism is stupid

I think it's hard not to have an element of racism. There's so much to process in the world that you categorise items to assist you in processing your information, and what is racism but a form of categorisation? So I understand that part. Here I go, I'm going to say something racist: I've found that when I encounter Russians, they tend to be curt. Now, I may have just been racist, but that is a personal observation based on my experience, and I should be able to share my experience. What is important is that when I meet another Russian, I give them time to be judged based on merit.

I have another theory on African and African American oppression that I explained to an American, and he cut me down, saying that it was racist. I'll explain afterwards. Let me start by saying that where I grew up is multicultural, but mainly European, then Asian, but not African until the last two decades where now we have more colour in our neighbourhoods. My experience in connecting with Africans and even First Nations people was rare. I did, however, love music – hip hop, soul, funk, punk, grunge – you name it, I love it. And many of its best practitioners are African Americans. I would love to attend a soul church to feel that vibe, like when James Brown takes services in the Blues Brothers. That would be a life highlight. But I'm unsure whether attending for entertainment or cultural experience purposes is disrespectful, so I wouldn't do it without consultation.

I have also seen Africans and African Americans play sports and dominate with their chiselled physiques. I've seen them dance like nobody is watching and move with such soul that it makes me feel robotic. I've seen them in space, arts and science. There's a common stereotype that their penises are meant to be larger, too. I think they are such an amazing example of humans and have a theory that the white European man's suppression of them was from intimidation, especially in the days when having better endurance held more weight. You would really want to control a more impressive version, to prevent them from overthrowing you.

So, I told this theory to a friend of mine's American friend. He told me that this is racism, too. I think they might call it positive racism. Anyway, he said that even though it's a positive view, there are African Americans with smaller penises or who can't dance or sing, so the positive racism doesn't help them. I think he has a point. But I still think I do, too, about Africans being intimidating to the Europeans and how that may have led to their enslavement. I think that in many ways they are finer examples of humans than Westerners. Is that racist too? I'm a little confused, and what has this to do with parenting? I think how we judge people should be merit-based. We live in a multicultural world and should be open to all cultures and races however different. We should teach our children the same; they will invariably be in classrooms, sport fields and workplaces with a variety of people and will need to respect and interact with them, so keep them open-minded and free of racism.

Watch 'Love on the spectrum'

If you haven't heard of this show, it started in Australia, and they've now made an American version. It should be shown in schools to all children. It follows young adults on the spectrum looking for love and dating. It talks to their friends and family. The contestants and their dates are interviewed along the way. To start with, I just love seeing people fall in love and always hope that it works out, so the romantic in me is gunning for the contestants the whole time. More importantly, it helped my son and me understand what spectrum and neurodivergence mean, how wide the spectrum is, and how to better interact, create an environment and make space for this condition. We delighted in watching this series, and I remember concluding that we are all on the spectrum. Pay the extra fee for a Netflix subscription and watch it with your children without commercials. It is an amazing example of how television can be a force for good and positive change.

Screens are communication

It's really a different world in which I was raised. Screens were limited to Saturday morning cartoons, and if you were lucky an Atari game system. What is consistent is that we look like zombies when we watch screens. The content has changed dramatically, and they are now interactive entertainment, information, and communication tools that we all must master to get by. I'm not convinced that they're as beneficial to developing interpersonal skills as 'ye olde' way of communicating. I find the tonality, content and expectations of the speed of response so nuanced and tangled in a web of yet-to-be-discovered rules. I generally avoid communicating through social media and limit myself to email, messaging and memes. I know, I'm a dinosaur.

It's a minefield out there for kids: posts where friends will disclose their feelings and obligatory responses are expected, with the threat of being ostracised if you don't. Kids are bullied, and it can be just awful out there. I liken it to road rage, where people go crazy in their cars within their safe barrier; however, if they were to run into people on the street, they would be kinder and more tolerant. But there's more to it than communication: information screaming at lightning speed, plans made, ideas shared, funds exchanged, worlds to conquer and creativity.

Us dinosaurs once bonded over the latest episode or a film; now we are laughing at the latest post, viral video or meme. High-school kids want to have a phone to be able to share and organise. I'm not sure how you can avoid this and still have them functioning in an adolescent world. I wish I had better advice in this area. I once saw a snippet of Gary Vee being asked by a parent on how she could protect her own daughter from it. His response was that as a father of a teenage daughter, he understands the situation too. His advice was to build self-esteem in the child from an early age. It takes an understanding of one's value to enable them to reject the nonsense and navigate the seas of social media, which is communication but so intense and nuanced.

Mealtime is sacred

We love food in my home. It's generally me making meals, and I put a lot of effort into them. It shows, too, because I just love feeding people. If my child put that much effort into a project, I would certainly give it the time it deserves, and it should be no different at mealtime. It's more than that, too – it's a place to explore ideas and share experiences on how the day went, deconstructing how issues, behaviours and tasks were handled. It's the planning over breakfast, checking in over lunch and a debriefing over dinner. It's the small talk which leads to big talk. It's a time to show that the house is a village, and the person who has taken the time to prepare the meal should not be the person to pack it away. It's a time to share, show respect and appreciation to the ones we love. Mealtime is the closest I get to being religious.

If you nail the boring stuff, that's life

This one came from Jordan Peterson, who I do not know much about aside from some articulate snippets of his interviews. I have been informed by a friend who despises him that he can be misogynistic, but I have no other basis for that, nor have I seen it in my cursory viewing of him talking. I will still steal a nugget of information from him irrespective of whether this is true. I saw him talking about 'the small stuff'. He said that life is not about getting holidays right or being able to party; this is but a brief amount of time in your life. The majority is meals with your loved ones, shopping, catching up with people and your work. If you get this right – the small bits that make up so much of your day – then you are eighty percent of the way to getting life right. It's the regular small stuff which is a bigger part of our day. Get those bits right and the rest will work itself out. So, make that breakfast time matter, laugh, do a quiz. We really love doing a quiz and playing Connections and

Wordle at the New York Times website most mornings – it's a ritual, and it's free. We never have a screen playing; maybe some music in the mornings to sing to. Get those everyday moments right, cherish them, and don't wait for them to be gone before you appreciate them.

Speak about the opposite sex as if you are speaking to your parent

This one came from when I was having lunch on the tailgate of a truck with a bunch of blokes on a film set. It came from Rory, one of the most handsome young males I have ever met. He is the lead singer of an up-and-coming band who are now very much on the rise. I am so proud of him. He is an all-round great human being and connects with his family, children and adults with care and love. So, the situation was six blokes eating lunch at the back of a film truck. The subject of one of the actress's physiques came up, and one of the guys said, 'She has great tits.' I noticed Rory dipping his head, turning around, and walking off. I approached him shortly afterwards and asked if he was offended by the conversation. He told me that he used to talk about women that way till his mid-teens, when he decided that it was crass and inappropriate. He'd made a conscious decision to never talk about women that way again. He would talk about women in a way in which he would talk about them to his mother. I thought it was a great barometer of what you should and shouldn't say.

All consensual sex is good

Who are we to judge? If it's consensual then let them have their kinks. Shibari, anal, gay sex, S&M, swinging, non-monogamous – whatever it is, it's up to the two or more people. There are a lot of other issues wrapped up in this. Are the people right-minded? Is someone manipulating the other? Let's just assume it's two right-minded people who have consented; let them explore, have fun and determine their own boundaries. Being open like this and letting your children know, will only keep the lines of communication open with them as they grow. If they have kinks, then they should not be shamed by them, and they will be more open to talking to you about issues that arise.

Ok, I remember there was a case in Germany where a man allowed another man to cut off his penis and shallow-fry it and eat it. Far out! That one is a doozy to unpack. In my opinion, if they were right-minded and consented, that is up to them and is their business. Just because you don't feel it, doesn't mean it's wrong. I think we should remove the stigma associated with kinks and keep our kids sex positive. You should let them know that different people do it in different ways, and it's about consent and boundaries, which means good communication is necessary – and communication is the best foreplay.

Mind your own business

I deplore gossip. I do think it's important to discuss issues in other families to deconstruct behaviours and responses. Knowing of others' misfortune or handling of experiences can help you consider the situation. It should be done with warmth and in a spirit of learning. I have heard people talking about movie stars like they know what's going on in their lives. Oh, please – you're a sucker if you think the snippets of information garnered from tabloids are representative of the people they write about. And who cares? Just mind your own business. This extends to what happens in the house. I share financial information and concerns about myself and others to my son, but I expect that this will stay within the vault. Minding your own business goes both ways, so when my son has informed me of information about other parents, I let him know that it is none of our business too.

Your beliefs are my beliefs, but they might change

I am a complete atheist and, in turn, so is my son, because that is my religion. Once we were driving and my son said, 'I will never believe in God,' so I stopped him immediately and let him know that the only reason he doesn't believe in God is because I don't believe in God, and he shouldn't be so final about that. He then responded with, 'I don't believe in God, and it's unlikely that I ever will.' I couldn't argue with that. I just don't think you should be so final about your beliefs – let children know that they have a choice. I think that's empowering, and should they gravitate toward a religion it will be of their own doing. Who knows? One day I might believe in God, but it's unlikely. I would really appreciate it if religious people said this to their children, rather than just indoctrinating them.

I also had a friend point out to me that if I have a Christian friend, they would want me to have eternal life, and if they truly loved me, that they would want to convert me. It made me think, because I predominantly deplore bible bashing; but the people who go door-to-door to convert people are possibly doing it because they love you, so maybe don't be too harsh to them. In their view, they are trying to save your soul. Politely let them know you appreciate their effort, but you are willing to be damned and to move on.

Perfection is so boring

So boring that I do not want to write about it.

It doesn't matter what you do, just do it well

So, I try to think that I've succeeded in being focused on the effort rather than the result. There have been some good results, and I think that's great. There have been some results that were not as good as my son expected, and that was fine too. Tests in the early years of secondary school, projects and exams are there to teach the child the process and how to best complete them to reflect their knowledge. My son is a slow writer, so that's not too helpful in exam conditions, but with all the practice he is getting better. I think you can shift the viewpoint regarding exams. Instead of looking at it as a test of knowledge, look at it as a test showing what you need to work on more to wholly understand the course material. That's important because the following years build on the basics of the subject. This shift from a result being a grade to an indication of what you need to work on is a significant one. You are more grateful for the indication of what you need to work on.

Their occupation options are vast and unknown

A common question I hear asked of children is, 'What do you want to be when you grow up?' The answer should be along the lines of, 'Adjusted and independent with a love of life, strong connections and financial stability.' But you normally get doctor, actor, singer, lawyer, surgeon, plumber or builder. Ok, plumber was a lie – no one wants to be a plumber. At one stage I mentioned to a friend that I thought being a plumber isn't too bad a job. His response was that eventually you'll get some shit in your mouth, and it's not going to be yours.

As usual, I'm digressing. The point I was trying to make is that there are thousands of occupations which aren't considered by kids. My day job, prior to retiring from the proceeds of sales from this book, is finding and managing locations for film and television. I've never heard of that listed as a prospective occupation by a kid. I have a friend who is a festival organiser. I know photographers, gaffers, radiologists and coffee roasters to name a few, and there are just so many more occupations to list.

From my experience, many friends didn't follow the path where their degrees were heading. I guess asking the question is interesting – to see where the child thinks that their interests and strengths are – but I think it's important to let them know that there is a world of occupations. I highly value education, but I think its importance is greater than a path to a specific occupation; more a path to knowledge to be used in a field, but which can be adapted to other areas. This is why I'm critical of my own education and would have appreciated more of an arts component to it, too.

Some subjects seem irrelevant, but they are not

Oh, where am I ever going to use this?' I know I'm guilty of this, and that's why it's here. It's hard to see the forest for the trees and appreciate why you are learning trigonometry, history of Russian politics, Westminster system, ratios, accounting... (Insert your subject here.) That is the folly of youth – concurrently the age where you are best able to learn but are naïve. Kids lack the vision to appreciate that they, like opportunities, will change, and having a breadth of knowledge will help them navigate this. So, give your child examples of how subjects you thought were padding become important; how understanding them helped you later in life. It was mainly accounting for me. Let them know that you made errors of judgement in relation to this. Hopefully they do not make the same or as many errors in judgement as you and me.

Continuous improvement and growth

You can talk about it, but if you aren't doing it yourself, it isn't a strong lesson. So, show your kids that even as an adult you get things wrong, change your opinions, pivot, learn and grow. I grew up in a time where there was no gay marriage, and I heard comments from more progressive elders that being gay was ok, but as long as they do it in private – and that was the progressive ones. If you are reading this book, I hope you are accepting that love is just that, and whichever gender is involved is irrelevant. That took time for the public to accept, and to think otherwise in my progressive bubble is nonsense.

As my friends and I approach fifty, I'm noticing that these 'progressive, pro-gay' friends are struggling to accept the exploration of gender and its variations along the spectrum. So, it's more like, 'I am fine with gays, but people identifying as a cat? What is the world coming to?' I, too, find it hard to grasp a human identifying as another species. I mean, I knew a disproportionate number of pubescent girls in my youth who thought they were a dolphin in a past life. For the record, I never met one who declared they are a less-adored animal in a previous life – maybe dolphins have better karma. Instead of being closed to these new parameters, I think it's best to have the position of, 'I don't understand it, but I am open to seeing where it's going.' If I get your pronouns wrong and you correct me, I am fine with that. If we have time, perhaps you can explain it to me. I also think that the people who identify with a different pronoun should take the time when available to explain the reasoning for its use to help educate the public. Wherever you lie on the spectrum, be open and friendly because you want your neighbour to say, 'Our gay/trans/poly/agender neighbours are so lovely, have great taste and make great mimosas.' This is where tolerance starts.

I had to remind my son, who has a strong sense of self, that personality is constantly developing, and that personality and beliefs are dynamic. The person you are at fifteen is not the person you are at twenty-five years of age. There is something joyous about that. It's the belief that a leopard does change its spots. That can extend to yourself and other people. People (and you) can get better, then worse and then better again. I find that comforting.

Be active

I just find following sports so boring, but I love playing them, especially tennis and pickleball. There is so much to be gained from sports, whether it's being part of a team or battling with your own self to push through. Physically, I believe it's unanimous that it helps in so many ways. I'm not going to labour this; let's accept that being active is all-round good for you. With the rise of constant content, it is easy to be inactive – not that taking a break and chilling is without value, but it's just a question of balance. Those screens can really suck you in, and if you love to get your fix of dopamine from screens, that's where you're going to go for it. But these lessons start at a young age. If you're appeasing your kids with screens early, it's passive entertainment. They are going to crave it later. Shooting hoops, hanging at the playground, going to the beach or spending a wonderful, long day at the beach or park is a great place to start. Working can be exhausting, and coming home and chilling is so tempting and sometimes necessary, but take time to be active during the week to show how important it is to your wellbeing.

Keep it tidy so you can find shit

I hate – and I don't use 'hate' often – looking for things. It may be because I lack patience, and I am terrible at it. I decided many years ago that if I can't find it easily, I'm not allowed to keep it. It's a double-edged sword: it is super convenient, but can make you a little rigid, potentially in my case adding to long-term bachelorhood. It's actually derived from Montessori – there's a principle that the younger children get to pick tasks called 'jobs'. They select any job they want to do for as long as they want to do it. The jobs are presented on trays, and once a job is complete or needs to be put away, it's returned to the tray and placed where it was found. Aside from the organisational benefits, it also teaches respect for the materials and courtesy in leaving items as they were found for the next student. A child's clothing, toys, books and bed are not disposable or replaceable items, but privileges which are to be respected with gratitude. Keep your home and the world tidy.

Adventure is awesome

There is so much to gain by adventuring. I'm talking about going on walks on cliffs, rock climbing, chasing waves, walking through a forest or walking across a river. It can get scary, but working through fears to accomplish something is rewarding, and is a good habit to instil. There's also the development of motor skills, making memories, bonding, enjoying of the outdoors, and being connected to nature. They don't have to be high-adrenaline activities – after all, kids are tiny – but their power-to-weight ratio is the best it will ever be, so let them take little risk. In fact, overdo the sense of danger just to add drama. And most importantly, have fun.

Do not answer for them

I have seen this so many times. I love engaging with kids. I have always had a natural connection with them. Up until a few years ago, I was always on the kids' table at Christmas, but that's changed with the current generation. The point I'm trying to make is that when I meet a kid, I like to talk to them – and talk to them like a person. Many times, if they are with their parents, the parents will answer for them when I am clearly talking to the child. I always correct the parent and let them know I am talking to the child. This wins points with the child, too. How are kids expected to be independent, have a voice and learn to communicate with all kinds of people if you answer for them? Don't do it. Let them learn. If they are too shy to answer, that's ok too. It's obvious. Hopefully they will grow out of it, but give them the opportunity.

They can find the toilet

Ok, maybe not toddlers, but if you are at a café, restaurant, museum, gallery or a similar place and they ask you where the toilet is, ask them to find out and let you know. It's a simple opportunity for them to develop more life skills. I know it might seem trivial, but this all goes to developing their independence. There are so many teaching opportunities. Get them to pay for the groceries; have them return the cups to the counter or carry groceries; get them to help with the preparing of meals and cleaning. Just get them to do things – and by do things, I mean problem-solve.

Be positive, righteous and thankful

One of my favourite films is Kelly's Heroes. It stars Clint Eastwood, Telly Savalas, Don Rickles and Donald Sutherland. It's so funny with lots of classic lines. Donald Sutherland's character 'Oddball' could be the best, but Don Rickles's 'Crapgame' character is a close second. Oddball in the film is a hippie trying everything to avoid the war, and his mantra was to be positive, righteous and thankful. A great motto to live by and ties in with the 'empathetic' component of the mission statement.

Being positive allows you to tackle hurdles on the right foot. Righteousness is making sure that you have integrity and ensuring that you treat yourself and others with care and respect. Thankful is being grateful for what you have and not worrying about what you do not have. I have this mantra printed and on my fridge.

Cultures are amazing

It is a wonder of the world to see how different influences and conditions affect cultures. In some ways the world seems to be more gentrified, but the differences are still apparent. Weather, access to foods, topography, founding fathers/mothers and religion have such an impact on these different pockets – it's fascinating to see. One of the most profound travel experiences I had was to India in my mid-twenties, and it absolutely shaped me into a better person, reframing what was important in life. I will always be grateful to Mother India.

Other cultures hold a mirror up to your own. You can see the positives and negatives of various aspects. I guess I went to India with the moral high ground, being from a wealthy Western background, only to find that we lack the richness of village life. Share this with your kids; let them know that there are variations in the way people live. Let them know that having the latest sneakers does not lead to happiness. Although some countries seem poor, they are richer than ours. Climbing the corporate ladder is not a pathway to happiness, but maybe helping people is? It also helps our children not to be racists, because racism (as previously mentioned) is stupid.

Art is amazing

How wonderful is creativity and talent? When it is combined with action, you get art. Not all of it might move you, but there's usually a piece which sticks with you. We have some art around our house. I would marvel at the brush strokes and how a simple flick of the brush created what appeared to be a boat on water. When travelling, I have witnessed some of the world's most famous paintings and sculptures and was in awe of their beauty. How wonderful it is to be moved and inspired.

I took some friends' children to the National Gallery of Victoria for an excursion. To the gallery's credit, they always have a kid-focused area to engage them. We saw the piece 'Comedian' by Italian artist Maurizio Cattelan. That is so great – it's a banana taped to a wall. Such a thought-provoking example of how art can be so varied and challenges the idea of what art can be, its portability, its endurance. It just is a banana taped to a wall; if you visit it two weeks later, it isn't going to be the same banana or the same tape, but it will be the same artwork. They loved it and other pieces. What I did do was not labour in any one area and to move through the gallery at their pace. I still need to revisit that exhibition again to go at my pace, but I was there for them and not for me.

Poor behaviour is worth deconstructing

This is about being judgmental, which isn't the greatest trait. But it's 'judgemental' in a manner to deconstruct. When returning from friends' homes or events, we would debrief in the car about what transpired; if there were bad habits or behaviours, we'd break them down. It was a good lesson on what was right and wrong, considering situationally what led to the behaviour. I think it helps kids read the room, and plan on how to manage the situations and how best to avoid absorbing those behaviours. I can be very judgmental of children, with a low tolerance for bad behaviours and a very direct way of letting them know. I think it's important to add to this that kids do change. I know I had to keep reminding my son that some of the behaviours were just part of their development – or maybe a better word is learning – and were not a lifelong attribute.

I am not your slave

Damn straight I am not your slave, and if you want to be brutal, your kids need you more than you need them. So do not let them rule. No-one should rule you. You call the shots; you decide if things are going to happen, and they are coming along for the ride. They need to take care of their spaces to your standards. These are the rules of the house that they live in. Your time is precious, and they need to contribute. They are part of your home, and you are all working towards the same goal. I have seen kids using sharp knives with speed and precision to help in the family restaurant and cook a meal for the family with confidence. They are capable – that's why there are child labour laws. I'm not proposing you get them to make fake Gucci purses, and I do hope you are finding the humour in my example. The point I'm making is that if you give them enough space to grow, they will grow into it. They need some guidance at the start, but let them work for their supper. I assure you: if they prepare their supper, they are more likely to eat it and not complain.

They're not sophisticated enough

Kids are not sophisticated. And I know I propose that they have independence and can lead, but the reality is that they don't know all the consequences. Even in early learning Montessori as I've explained, they're free to make their own decisions – however, their options are curated. Whether it's food, leisure, family occasions, schooling or sleep time, you need to manage how this time is spent. I had the tricky situation that my son loved to hug and kiss his parents and a select few friends when he was a toddler, but didn't want to hug or kiss other people. We would visit my Zia (Auntie) Conchetta only a few times a year, so she was familiar to my son, but not very close, but I insisted he had to kiss her hello and goodbye. He didn't want to do it. It was a challenging thing, but it was non-negotiable and culturally necessary. To be honest, I didn't like forcing him to do it, but in retrospect I'm so glad that I made him. It was a bigger issue than it needed to be – a small discomfort on his behalf to show respect for his elders. Learning that he must do things which he doesn't want to do, for the benefit of others in certain circumstances, is an important lesson. You could equally argue that my forcing him to kiss his great aunt is turning him into a pleaser going against his will. It was a difficult position to take and took an unreasonable amount of effort to push the idea, but I am glad in retrospect: the kissing of our relatives is part of the Italian culture and a sign of respect.

Walking is great

The Italians call it a 'passeggiata'. It's a walk you go for after a meal, often through the piazza with a stop at the gelato shop. You cannot fault those Italians for culture and food. Whether it's after dinner or during the day, going for a walk promotes conversation, aids in digestion, is a great way to observe the world and helps with getting to know your neighbourhood and community. I would have friends over on a Sunday night for dinner for many years when my son was a toddler. It was the same group of friends every week, plus some special guests on the odd occasion. After dinner we would walk, talk and laugh around the block. We all valued the Sunday meal and passeggiata together.

I follow @glucosegoddess* a.k.a Jessie Inchauspé, a biochemist on Instagram, and she also promotes the walk after meals based on science. It's interesting when long-time cultural patterns are proven to have physiological benefits.

* https://www.glucosegoddess.com/

Swimming is a joy

My mother was born on a very small Italian island – which is the world's most active volcano – with perfect water. Australia is an island where we predominantly live along the perimeter, so water and swimming is part of the fabric of our family and of who I am. I rarely travel without the option to be able to visit a beautiful beach or body of water, and my son has the same draw to water. In a world where activities are often planned, curated and paid for, you can always pack a bag and drive down to the beach and have one of the best days free of expense.

I remember looking out at the ocean on a hot summer's day and seeing adults talking and sunbaking on the sand and kids playing on the shoreline building sandcastles, along with elderly people, toddlers and babies in the shallows. Kids and teenagers at waist depth throwing balls and frisbees. A couple of lovers a little deeper and surfers out the back waiting for a set to come in. All these people of varying age demographics and psychographics all having just a great day at no financial cost. The beach is a great leveller; there's no class system on the beach, and we are all the same and have the same entitlement to it. The freedom for Australians to utilise the beach is part of our culture – we find it confronting when we travel and there are private beaches.

So, in Australia, not being able to swim is unusual. Many of us take our kids to swim lessons, because culturally it is part of us and one of my favourite things to do – my happy place.

Listening is a skill

We were taught this at business school, but I am unsure as to why it's not taught at primary school. There is so much to be gained by just observing and absorbing. There's a saying I heard once: better to be thought of as a fool than to open your mouth and remove all reasonable doubt. I'm not sure how pertinent that saying is here, because the last thing I want kids to be taught is 'to be seen and not heard'. They should have a voice and be heard. They just need to learn to listen.

So much can be gained from listening. It allows observations of the non-verbal communication in addition to the verbal. Kids are sponges, and I've seen the crafty ones quietly absorbing adult conversations whilst pretending to do something else. I love those smart little kids, and I always send them a smile to let them know that I know what they are doing. This should be extended to when you are having conversations – they should wait for a natural pause. If they interrupt, let them know that you'll get to them after you've finished. It's important to remember to give them your attention after the conversation reaches a natural pause, but make them wait.

I saw a snippet of the cartoon Bluey. I've never watched an episode, but I hear it's fantastic. In the snippet, the father explained that if he is talking to someone, his child only needs to touch his hand, and the father will acknowledge the touch by placing his hand over his child's hand. The father will respond to her once there's a break in the current conversation, and the parent must do this, as it builds trust and confidence for the next time they want to get your attention. That is a great lesson to teach a child.

Books are valuable

I loved reading to my son, and he loved being read to. Once he was able to read by himself, his love of books continued. I never read Harry Potter, but my son did, but I think they have been invaluable in encouraging young people to continue reading. The slow absorption of a story is such a wonderful experience. I think it would be better if they read the books before they see the films, as the film already paints a picture of the characters and the scenes, whereas reading it fresh allows the reader to paint the picture.

I once heard the question being discussed as to what the greatest form of art is. The initial argument I heard was music because it's abstract, universal and makes you move, and you feel it through your body. It's a strong argument. Later I heard someone respond with writing, because it allows the author to get in the head of a reader in that very personal space where the internal monologue resides. I thought that was a remarkable suggestion. I hadn't thought of it like that before.

Reading helps with communication and literacy. It makes the reader learn from other people's perspectives, shares information and transports them to another world. A great story is engaging and sits with you for a long time. There are so many great kids' books. Some of our favourites were Everybody Poos, We're Going on a Bear Hunt, The Illustrated Odyssey, Where the Wild Things Are and Who Sank the Boat? I recently bought these for my great-nephew, and my son glowed at seeing the titles and remembering how much he loved the stories.

Investing is important

I am grouping investing and saving together, because I think that they go hand in hand. It can start early – in fact, we started at the age of five where I started giving my son $200 per month. When it grew to $1,000, we would buy a share on the stock market and follow its trajectory. I made some risky speculative purchases. Some paid off, but many have not. In retrospect I really should have stuck with the big companies like Apple, Tesla, Nvidia, Amazon and Disney, or an EFT. They are no-brainers; being part of such great organisations is a safe bet long-term, and investing with hindsight is a lot easier. The important thing was explaining compound interest and that saving $1,000 dollars at 10% this year meant he would have close to $1,100 in a year, $1,210 the year after and compounding onwards. Also, I told him that continually saving even small amounts meant that he could easily afford a deposit on a house in his late twenties. It also works the other way: spending $100 now is going to cost you an extra $10 this year and $11 the year after. The truth is that giving him this money at an early age is just a way for me to save for his future big purchases, whilst allowing him to see the value of saving, and the power of small, incremental compound growth.

It also changes the way you look at money. Know that if you spend $10,000 on a couch, it's still going to cost you at a 10 percent gain – about $1,000 a year by not saving that money, or $20 a week. The following year the couch is going to cost you $1,100 a year or $22 a week. I know it's a simple example, but it blows my mind.

Cooking is fun

Cooking is fun – maybe not as much as eating. And let's face it, cleaning blows. But it's all part of the process. Great times can be had cooking together with your child or with your partner or friends. It's a great bonding experience, made even better with some good music.

Cooking is science – mixing, measuring, heating, experimenting – and you get to eat the results. It's technical, passionate and dangerous, too. What a combination. If a child cooks, it would have to be bad for them not to eat it. There is so much to be gained from the experience. It shows how much effort goes into preparing food, and aids in memory, motor skills, self-esteem and independence and contributes to the village. If your child is hungry, they should be able to cook up an egg at least or cut themselves some fruit. It will take longer and be messier, but it's such an important skill, and the complexity of the recipes can increase with time. How exciting.

Contributing is awesome

Everyone wins when kids contribute. Doing everything for them is not helping them. It's your job to prepare them for adulthood. Furthermore, they will value the house more and feel like part of the team. I do feel like I have covered this already.

Wear what you want

Do not let social conventions control what you or your child wears. I don't even let the weather affect what they wear. Let them work it out. If they're cold or hot, they will work it out. Let them adjust. Remember: you do not catch a cold from cold air – please remind the Italians who are still afraid of a breeze. If your son wants to wear a dress, a pink outfit or a rainbow flag, or your daughter just likes overalls, who cares? Let them be an individual. Conforming is so boring, and being comfortable is the best. They will work out that they should have taken a jumper with them – you can even suggest it – but unless you are in an extreme climate, let them work it out and save yourself the stress.

Be cool

'Cool' is such an ambiguous term, but I rate it as so important. To be cool means to be kind, individual, open, interesting and adventurous, so cool is everything to me. Cool is not wearing expensive clothes, being rude to people or being narrow-minded or pretentious. Everybody should be way cooler.

Media is pretend – make a movie

I love movies and great TV shows. Hell, I even love bad TV shows. But it's all make-believe. They are stories, and remember: 'reality TV' is the most orchestrated of them all. It's good to know this at an early age. For my son's first birthday I made a short movie of him spinning records and riding skateboards. It didn't win any awards, but it's a great memento of his first year. It really shows how fictitious film can be. We even comment how special effects in films are just like that 'wild strawberries' video of ours. So, when we watch an action film, we know that they're just stories. If you want to see our masterpiece online, go to YouTube and search for 'Skateboarding Wild Strawberries PNAU'.

Silence is wonderful

A break in talking or noise should be welcomed. We spend so much time together that it's not necessary to fill those moments with conversation, music, or the TV in the background. I don't know many people I can spend a lot of time with and maintain an interesting conversation, so be comfortable with silence. I have a friend who always has the TV on irrespective of what's on. It pains me, but that is what he likes. Personally, being quiet in the house is a blessing and a good time to relax, reflect or to work on a project.

Nature is stunning

There is so much to love about nature. I was given a book called If I Could Tell You Just One Thing...: Encounters with remarkable people and their most valuable advice by Richard Reed. In this book they interviewed many notable people, and Sir David Attenborough's advice was along the lines of, 'Children love nature, and as you become an adult, don't lose the love and amazement of nature.' I think it's such great advice. You can look across a wide panorama and see the landscape, and then look to your toes where there is so much activity in the earth underfoot: winds blow, birds are looking for food, trees are growing and adapting to their environment. Observe the flora changing as you walk along. There is so much drama in nature, and its harmony is breathtaking – stop to look around.

Be a rebel

This advice is more for the kids than the adults, so adults, look away and pass this page to your kids. I have written it in small font so only young eyes can see it.

You don't have to do what you are told. Question people, especially adults and teachers. You can make your own mind up and carve your own path. Adults are paper tigers: they may appear scary, but they are not. You are the future – do not let them push you around with their antiquated ideas.

It was from writing this book that I unlocked a very old memory of reading a banned book in my late teens called The Little Red School Book by Søren Hansen and Jesper Jensen. It was a book presented to me in my late teens with the information that it was written in the 1970s and had been banned, and that I shouldn't be reading it. So its allure was strong. It's from this book I picked up that adults are 'paper tigers'. It was only through some googling that I was able to find this book again. Upon reflection, I'm realising how impactful this book was on my life. I was a rebellious teen, and this book only fuelled this rebellion. I think this book I'm writing is inadvertently a homage to The Little Red School Book.

I have since purchased this book though Amazon and shared it with my son. He was amused at the content, some of it obvious and reflective of the conversations we've had about important and controversial topics. I think we have opened up a lot from the 70's, and perhaps this book helped a little – it certainly did for me.

Question adults

Adults have learned a lot, but they can also be rigid, thinking they have worked it out, which is their major downfall. But ideas and life are dynamic. I always thought that children are the new, improved version of the adult, ready to learn new ideas and grow.

You know when you go to the supermarket and the laundry powder you used to buy is a little different, and is now 'new and improved'? That's what our kids should be.

Co-sleep

I just loved co-sleeping. Whenever my son slept with me, he would always have part of him touching me, no matter how he moved and positioned himself in the bed. There was the security of having his parent(s) there. We are so vulnerable when we sleep that having a protector close by is so comforting. I just don't understand that a baby who has been so connected to a mother and then ejected from the comfort of a womb would want to be isolated in their own bed – to me that's just not natural. My bed is always open to my son. He wanted to sleep in his own bed eventually, but he always had, and still has a safe space to come to. I know that there are arguments about rolling over on a child. I was always acutely aware that I was in bed with my child, and you should not be inebriated when sleeping with a child; that is just foolish.

Don't be kid-bombed

It is everybody's house, and the mountains of toys discarded across the living room are too much. Birthdays and Christmas only add to the toy landscape. I was a single parent who dates a lot, so that was a big motivation to keep my house from being kid-bombed. It's more than that – kids can have their room, but the house is for the family. Also, the toys need to be valued, which includes using them, enjoying them and then packing them away, so you know where they are next time you want to use them. It shows respect for the toys and respect for the house.

Overstimulation is a problem

There is so much going on from adverts on TV on bus stops to devices vying for their attention – it's all a bit much, and it wouldn't be surprising to hear attention spans have declined. Part of keeping a neat house and having things in order is to reduce distractions and allow time to focus on one task. I'm not sure how school is meant to compete with the flashiness of YouTube, TikTok or Instagram.

Trust

I purposely left trust till the end. So much of how connected I am with my son, and how easy parenting has been for me, comes from trust. If you trust each other in your words and actions, then you will both be on the same page. I talked about being honest previously, especially when it comes to the harder stuff like talking about drugs and sex. By being open with your child, you are building trust together. By letting them know about your foibles, they understand you better. Trust helps me understand that when my son makes a mistake, is late or breaks something, I know –and he knows that I know – that he did it accidently, and there was no malice behind it. When my son was on the other side of the world on student exchange and his host father said some nasty things about his role in the home, I knew that when I spoke to my son, he was telling the truth and that the father was lying. I have let my son know that this trust we've built manifests into the many privileges he has including being able to stay out late, being free and having opportunities and experiences. It means that he has told me when he's been exposed to drugs and alcohol. It means that we see and talk to each other; we know we are on the same team. It's a beautiful thing, and even though my son is a pleaser, I am a pleaser, too, and we are trying to support each other to be the best people we can be.

I hope that my advice, albeit naïve and void of any academic credentials, helps you build this trust with your child, so you can have a wonderful relationship with them. They have so much to offer. They make us accountable and make us reflect on our past and how we can be better. I am so grateful for the parenting experience.

I lament my situation of getting a woman pregnant who I was not in love with as not one of my best performances. I don't like regret, as regret is presuming the alternative was better, which is a hopeful assumption. But I have never regretted being a parent. I am a better man because of it.

With thanks

So, I've never written a book before, but I thought I'd give it a try. The way you see it is how I came up with it. I made a note of all the things I wanted to cover as a heading and then wrote about each one. There is no narrative, and as I kept going, I felt like I started to repeat myself at times – and to be honest, towards the end I started to tire of the project and want to get it out there, so the chapters get briefer and there may be a little repetition. I'm sorry to say I have more to cover, but let's see how this one goes. If there's a large petition or public protest demanding a second book, well... you never know.

I did not make this with any expectations other than to make it. If one day my son can read it and get an idea as an adult of my beliefs and why I did things a certain way for him, that will be enough. I hope he takes what he likes, rejects the rest, becomes a better parent than me, and has kids who are not dicks.

Maybe I will have to recant everything when my son ends up a junkie in jail. Although I'm doing my very best to be a good parent, it's no guarantee that my son will be a great man. I think about this: I think he is incredible and has the best start in life I could give him, but the rest is up to him.

www.ingramcontent.com/pod-product-compliance
Lightning Source LLC
LaVergne TN
LVHW012116170826
845678LV00014BA/2953

* 9 7 8 0 6 4 6 8 9 3 3 8 9 *